Piano Solo

The James Booker C

CONTENTS

All titles are on the CD (Hannibal HNCD 1359), except:

Come Rain or Come Shine, Tell Me How Do You Feel–New Orleans Piano Wizard: Live!—CD: Rounder CD 2027

Papa Was a Rascal—CD: Resurrection of the Bayou Maharajah (Rounder CD 2118)

Gonzo's Blue Dream—CD: Spiders on the Keys (Rounder CD 2119)

Cover Photo: Michael Smith

ISBN 0-7935-9337-9

7777 W. BLUEMOUND RD. P.O. BOX 13819 MILWAUKEE, WI 53213

Visit Hal Leonard Online at
www.halleonard.com

2

About James Booker

James Carroll Booker III was born in New Orleans on December 17, 1939. He was classically trained on piano from the age of six, at which time his astounding talents were already evident, and he was considered a child prodigy. He found his way into the local music scene as a young teenager, recording his first single, "Doin' the Hambone," at fourteen. Although it failed commercially, Booker got extensive studio work as a result, including uncredited 'ghost' piano tracks for Fats Domino. Throughout high school, Booker played regularly with many local and regional bands, while still maintaining an excellent academic record.

After graduating, Booker hit the road with Joe Tex, and spent the next several years gigging with various bands, including Earl King, Dee Clark and Huey 'Piano' Smith and the Clowns (actually replacing Huey, who preferred not to tour). In 1960, Booker recorded what would be his most commercially successful song, the organ-driven instrumental "Gonzo." Despite reaching number 10 on the Billboard R&B charts, the single failed to spawn a successful solo career for Booker, who spent the rest of the decade backing up many obscure acts and several better-known ones, including Wilson Pickett and Aretha Franklin.

In 1970, Booker was arrested on drug charges, and went to prison for several years. Upon his release, he spent some moderately successful years in New York and Los Angeles. He performed and recorded with such diverse artists as Ringo Starr, T-Bone Walker, Jerry Garcia, Lionel Hampton and even Dr. John, who'd been an informal student of Booker's several years earlier. At some point during this period, he lost his left eye. There are varied stories as to how this happened: a street fight over a financial dispute, a prison brawl, or the use of a dirty syringe. Ultimately no one knows for sure.

Booker returned to New Orleans in 1975, and played a highly successful solo set at the Jazz and Heritage Festival that same year. That performance proved to be a turning point in his career, leading to a European tour and a recording contract with Island Records. The resulting album, *Junco Partner*, featured Booker in top form, showcasing his talents on a solo piano and vocal set that includes originals, standards, R&B covers, and even his take on a Chopin waltz. Although the albums's sales were limited, it was critically acclaimed both domestically and abroad, and announced the presence of a major talent.

Booker made many European tours in the late seventies, cutting a handful of live albums which are regarded as his best recorded work. His blistering performance at the 1977 Boogie Woogie and Ragtime Piano Contest in Zurich is captured on the CD *New Orleans Piano Wizards: Live!* Two equally outstanding albums made during this period for German labels are now out of print.

After returning from Europe in 1978, Booker took a turn for the worse. His drug problem, which he'd controlled for several years, came back in full force. With the return of the habit came erratic behavior and paranoia. Local folklore is rife with stories of him passing out onstage, soliciting drugs from the audience, and stopping in mid-song to rant about the CIA, to name but a few tamer examples. In 1982, he recorded what would be his last album, *Classified,* which, despite some fine moments, lacks the brilliance of his earlier work.

He seemed to be getting himself together by 1983. He played regular gigs, worked a day job at New Orleans City Hall, and gave occasional piano lessons to another local child prodigy named Harry Connick, Jr. But on November 8, 1983, Booker suffered what appeared to be heart and lung failure, and died while awaiting attention at a local hospital.

The past few years have seen an increased awareness of Booker and his importance. His popularity has been boosted by the praise of a number of well-known pianists who were influenced by him, including Harry Connick, Jr., Dr. John, jazz/funk multi-keyboardist John Medeski and new age pioneer George Winston. The release of several previously unavailable recordings and a two hour radio documentary have made more of his music accessible than ever before, and his original songs have recently been performed and recorded by such contemporary bands as the Afghan Whigs and Medeski Martin & Wood. Booker may one day receive the kind of worldwide recognition that he always sought, but never found in his lifetime.

About the Music

James Booker was arguably the most accomplished pianist in the history of New Orleans rhythm and blues. In order to understand his unique piano style, it's necessary to look at his musical background. Obviously, he had assimilated the styles of related pianists who came before him, from New Orleans and elsewhere. In his playing you can hear echoes of the bent stride of Jelly Roll Morton, the Chicago blues of Pinetop Smith, the rhythmic innovations of Professor Longhair, the triplet bounce of Fats Domino, and, in particular, the R&B/gospel fusion of Ray Charles and Aretha Franklin, whom he cited as his two biggest influences. Also, though not a proficient modern jazz player, Booker understood the advanced harmonics of jazz, and used them to give his playing added harmonic strength and motion.

What really set Booker apart, however, were two advantages not shared by most pianists of his genre: serious classical training and great proficiency on the organ. As a child, he was earnest in his classical studies. His high school band director was the noted jazz pianist Ellis Marsalis, who recalls a teenage Booker playing Bach pieces at a professional level during school assemblies. His repertoire also included both straight renditions and his own reworkings of pieces by Chopin, Beethoven, Rachmaninoff and Cuban composer Ernesto Lecuona. On the organ, Booker was a strong "pedal player"; that is, he was able to play a bass line on the foot pedals while playing a melody with his right hand and a chordal accompaniment with his left. (Although his organ playing was rarely recorded, the recently released 2-CD set *United Our Thing Will Stand* offers a glimpse at his mastery of the instrument.) The common thread between his classical training and his organ skills is the concept of playing multiple, distinct parts simultaneously. Most blues-oriented pianists never develop this skill, but between the frequent polyphony of his classical repertoire and the multi-limb demands of the organ, Booker cultivated it to such an extent that it became a crucial element of his playing. By combining this ability with his knowledge of R&B piano styles and jazz harmonies, he synthesized a wholly unique piano sound, rich in texture, fluid in motion and greater than the sum of its parts.

Most of Booker's playing can be classified into seven different styles: a stride style, a funk style, an altogether different funk style based on stride, a ballad style, a rock style, a shuffle style and the ubiquitous Booker groove. We'll look at each of these individually.

The Booker Groove

The style most associated with Booker is one in which he played both a bass line and a chordal accompaniment with his left hand, while playing a melody with his right. This was usually a medium-tempo, straight-eighth note R&B, but could sometimes take on different rhythmic feels and tempos. Since its versatility makes it difficult to label as a specific musical genre, it's usually referred to simply as "the Booker groove." George Winston, in his liner notes to the *Junco Partner* CD, suggests that this style grew out of Booker's efforts to make the piano emulate the sound of the organ, with the left hand playing both the droning bass line of the pedals and off-beat chords of the lower manual.

Booker used many different combinations of bass lines and accompaniments when playing in this style. The most basic version appears in "Tico Tico," a song not printed here but available in the book *New Orleans Piano Legends:*

Although it's written as only one voice for readability, in order to get the proper rhythmic pulse you should think of the bass and accompaniment separately, like this:

The bass line should be slightly louder than the accompaniment, and there should always be a slight accent on beats 2 and 4. Also, the accompaniment usually anticipates chord changes, changing on the upbeat rather than the downbeat (as in the change from Am to E7 above). When this happens, the anticipated chord should get a slight accent.

In that example, the bass and accompaniment don't overlap rhythmically; the left hand is always playing one or the other, but not both together. In "Let's Make a Better World," the bass and accompaniment move together in parallel octaves:

(Written in two voices for clarity)

This happens again, with a triplet feel, in "Pop's Dilemma."

While these octaves aren't difficult to play, the difficulty increases significantly when the two parts overlap *and* move independently of one another, as in "Junco Partner":

In learning this type of pattern, it's useful to play the bass line and the accompaniment separately from one another before attempting to play them at the same time. Use the same fingering you would while playing them together.

The left-hand part of "Pixie" essentially consists of a single two-bar figure that moves among three different tonal centers:

With a fairly small hand span and only one overlapping note between the bass and accompaniment, this figure doesn't look especially difficult on paper. However, the syncopation in the second bar makes it surprisingly tricky, and keeping it going steadily—against the counter-syncopations of the right hand, and at Booker's tempo and level of swing—is a substantial chore. The best approach is to learn it much slower than the recorded tempo, taking care to play the rhythms accurately and maintain a relaxed swing feel. Increase the tempo only after you're very comfortable with the rhythms; it's better to play it slow and make it swing that to play it fast and have it sound clunky.

Much of Booker's music requires initially awkward-seeming leaps and stretches of the fingers (and mind). Once you're comfortable with them, however, it becomes apparent that they're the most logical, efficient way of getting the biggest possible sound from the piano. We can see this in the difficult variation of the Booker groove used in the intro and solo on "Come in My House":

It involves several tricky leaps, constant melodic motion, and both parallel and contrary movement between the bass line and accompaniment, all at a sweat-inducing tempo. While it doesn't have the rhythmic complexity of "Pixie," the sheer acrobatics required to wrap your fingers around the right notes make it a formidable challenge. Here again, slow practice is the key. (Booker also used this figure and the melody that goes against it in some versions of his original, "One Helluva Nerve.")

"Papa Was a Rascal" is the magnum opus of this collection, with several different stylistic approaches, long interludes between sections, a rubato verse and melodic quotes from assorted other songs. It contains a number of variations of the Booker groove, the most advanced occurring during the "St. Louis Blues" quote:

The continual melodic development in both voices makes this sound particularly like a two-handed figure, and makes it all the more startling when played with another melody on top of it. Check out the other bass line/accompaniment variations in this piece, and notice how each one provides a slightly different rhythmic push.

Several other pianists have adapted their own versions of the Booker groove. You can hear it in a great many of Dr. John's recordings—for starters, try "Big Mac" and "Saints." George Winston features his version heavily on his album of Vince Guaraldi music, especially on the cuts "Linus & Lucy," "The Masked Marvel" and "Treat Street." Harry Connick, Jr.'s version can be heard on "Bayou Maharajah" (a tune dedicated to Booker, with a brief melodic quote from "Come in My House") and "Avalon" (where he combines the Booker groove with Professor Longhair's rhumba rhythm).

Stride

Booker's approach to stride piano was fairly unusual. The typical left-hand technique in stride is to play low-register notes, octaves or chords on beats 1 and 3, and higher chords on beats 2 and 4:

Instead, Booker anticipated the notes on 1 and 3 with partial chords on the preceding upbeats:

This in itself isn't so uncommon, but what made Booker's approach to it unusual was his way of voicing these chords. Here are some of his voicings from "Keep on Gwine":

Here again, these notes will seem awkward to play at first, but they create a very distinct, full sound. Try substituting simple octaves or fifths and the song will sound anemic in comparison.

While playing stride, Booker usually played his right-hand melodies in block chords spanning an octave. While these can be tricky to play, Booker knew how to voice them economically, to get the most sound out of the least hand motion. Whenever possible, he kept the inner voices of a chord constant while moving only the outer voices. We can see this in "Keep on Gwine":

Another skill that Booker used to great effect in his stride playing was his ability to keep the time rock solid in his left hand while playing way behind the beat in his right. While this obviously isn't practical to notate on paper, it is an important part of his sound, and should be taken into account when playing these pieces. Listen to the recordings and notice where he keeps the time straight, where he lays it back, how far and what effect this has on the feel of the music.

Another great example of Booker's stride style is his rendition of "On the Sunny Side of the Street." Harry Connick, Jr. also recorded a Bookerish version of that song, and further shows the influence of Booker's stride playing on "After You've Gone."

Ballads

Booker's ballad style resembled a slowed-down, embellished version of his stride style. We can see this in the left hand of "Gonzo's Blue Dream" (which borrows its structure and overall feel from Ray Charles's "Sweet Sixteen Bars"):

The song is written in $\frac{6}{8}$ time because of its slow triplet feel, but if it's written in $\frac{4}{4}$ (with implied triplet eighth notes)...

...it looks virtually identical to one of Booker's stride patterns, except for the grace notes. Sometimes he would eliminate the lead-in notes for a less embellished effect, as in "Until the Real Thing Comes Along":

To build tension in ballads, Booker would sometimes switch from the slow triplet feel to a bouncy waltz-like feel. This happens in "Baby, Won't You Please Come Home":

And again, in a more complex variation, in "Come Rain or Come Shine":

It's important to note that Booker stretched the time further in ballads than in any other type of piece, dragging the tempo in some spots, pushing it in others, playing behind the beat in one hand or the other, and sometimes playing out of metric time altogether. In those instances, his rhythms have been "rounded off" to the closest possible metric division, but aren't notated exactly, because they can't be. Therefore, it's especially vital to listen to the recordings of these songs to get a true feel for how Booker played them.

Other excellent ballads from Booker's catalogue include "Please Send Me Someone to Love," "Let Them Talk," and "Black Night" (in which the piano part is inspired by Aretha Franklin's "Dr. Feelgood"). For another interesting comparison, listen to Dr. John's Booker-inspired version of "Come Rain or Come Shine."

Funk

Booker has a distinctly New Orleans-flavored funk piano style that involved playing a bass line in octaves with his left hand, while his right hand played a complex pattern reminiscent of Stevie Wonder or Sly Stone's two-fisted Clavinet riffs. The quintessential example of this is the main riff in "Papa Was a Rascal," which sounds like two hands playing this:

In reality, the right hand plays the whole thing, with the first two fingers serving as the "left hand" and the last three serving as the "right hand," while the (actual) left hand plays the bass line:

To maintain the proper feel, be sure to observe which notes are staccato and which are legato.

The version transcribed here was played at a moderate tempo (about 145 b.p.m.). Booker sometimes played this song faster, making it sound almost jaunty, and at other times quite a bit slower, giving it a nastier, gutter-funk feel. Try it at different tempos to see where it feels right.

Part of "Come in My House" features Booker's funk style as well:

He also sometimes played "Junco Partner" in this style, usually in B♭ rather than G.

Stride-Funk

Booker had another funk style, quite different from the first, which was derived from the stride concept. While the right hand plays the melody, the left hand provides the pulse of a kick drum with low-register octaves or partial chords, and a snare drum with middle-register chords. This is represented here in "Put out the Light":

For readability, this is written in double-time relative to the actual rhythmic pulse. When you play it, think of it in half time, with the "kick drum" notes on 1 and 3 (sometimes "1-and" and "3-and"), and the "snare" notes on 2 and 4, like this:

Note that this style frequently uses the same type of anticipations that appear in Booker's traditional stride style. Accent both the kick and snare notes (not the anticipations), and play them somewhat detached.

Booker didn't play in this style often, but you can hear it again in the "Slow Down/Boney Maroney" medley on the album *Resurrection of the Bayou Maharajah*. Harry Connick, Jr. used it on his rendition of "Winter Wonderland," but the pianist who has done the most with it by far is Henry Butler. Check out his "Orleans Inspiration" to hear a stride-funk tour de force.

Rock

The pulse for Booker's rock (or at least, rock-ish) style comes from a nearly unbroken stream of eighth notes in the left hand. Frequently these were octaves, either played together, staggered or a combination of the two. Usually when rock pianists play staggered-octave bass lines, the lower octaves occur on the downbeats and the upper octaves on the upbeats; however, often as not, Booker would turn this around and hit the upper octaves on the downbeats, creating a more tense feeling of motion. This happens in "Come in My House."

He would also sometimes substitute a tenth for the upper octave, alternate octaves with tenths, or play both the upper octave and the tenth together. We can see all of these in "Blues Minuet":

This piece is also notable for its intro, which Booker described as "counterpoint with one hand":

Shuffle

Booker didn't often play a straight-ahead boogie woogie shuffle, but when he wanted to, he could tear it up with the best of them. The prime example of this is "Tell Me How Do You Feel" (which borrows heavily from "Pinetop's Boogie Woogie" and from Huey Smith's piano part in Frankie Ford's "Roberta"). Again, the pulse came from steady left-hand eighth notes, played with a strong triplet feel. For these, Booker alternated between two approaches. One was simply to play staggered octaves, this time with the lower octaves on the downbeats. The other involved an altered version on this common boogie woogie bass line:

Booker added extra notes above the upper notes to create a fuller sound:

He added another twist too: rather than simply switching from one chord to the next, as most boogie woogie players do, he would play three-note lines leading into the next chord:

This creates added harmonic interest and keeps the song moving forward. Again, take care to maintain a solid shuffle feel and accent beats 2 and 4, as well as any anticipated chord changes.

More of Booker's shuffle style can be heard on his "Life/Wine Spo-Dee-O-Dee/It Should Have Been Me" medley from *Resurrection of the Bayou Maharajah*. Also, Dr. John recorded a version of "Pinetop's Boogie Woogie" (retitled "Pinetop") which he said he learned from Booker, and which has much in common with this cut.

For Further Reading

More detailed accounts of Booker's life can be found in the books *I Hear You Knockin'* by Jeff Hannusch, and *Up from the Cradle of Jazz* by Jason Berry, Jonathan Foose and Tad Jones. Also the liner notes to several of Booker's CD's contain valuable insights into his playing and personality. The *Junco Partners* liners feature some of Booker's own inimitable prose and musical analysis by George Winston. *Classified* offers bits of conversation between Booker and music journalist Bunny Matthews in its liner notes. Finally, *Spiders on the Keys* and *Resurrection of the Bayou Maharajah* both feature extensive commentary by various people who knew Booker—friends, managers and fellow musicians.

James Booker Additional Recordings

Classified (Rounder CD 2036)

King of the New Orleans Keyboard (Junco partner JP1)

The Lost Paramount Tapes (DJM CD 10010)

United Our Thing Will Stand (Night Train International NTI CD 2005)

For a complete Booker discography, go to:
http://offbeat.com/booker

Related Artist Discography

Henry Butler
Orleans Inspiration (Windham Hill WD-0122)
    "Orleans Inspiration"

Harry Connick, Jr.
20 (Columbia CK-44369)
    "Avalon"
25 (Columbia CK-53172)
    "After You've Gone"
Harry Connick, Jr. (Columbia CK-40702)
    "On the Sunny Side of the Street"
Lefty's Roach Soufflé (Columbia CK-46223)
    "Bayou Maharajah"
When Harry Met Sally (Sony CK-45319)
    "Winter Wonderland"

Dr. John
The Brightest Smile in Town (Clean Cuts 707)
    "Come Rain or Come Shine"
Dr. John Plays Mac Rebennack (Clean Cuts 705)
    "Big Mac"
    "Saints"

George Winston
Linus & Lucy: The Music of Vince Guaraldi (Windham Hill 11184)
    "Linus & Lucy"
    "The Masked Marvel"
    "Treat Street"

JUNCO PARTNER

By ROBERT ELLEN and MACK ELLEN

COME RAIN OR COME SHINE

from ST. LOUIS WOMAN

Words by JOHNNY MERCER
Music by HAROLD ARLEN

Ballad
slowly, rubato

GONZO'S BLUE DREAM

By JAMES BOOKER

Cadenza

LET'S MAKE A BETTER WORLD

By EARL JOHNSON

ev - er peo - ple shout, you got - ta hear 'em out. Ev - 'ry - bod - y is a beau - ti - ful

soul.

We got to pull to - geth - er,

hand in hand._____ We real - ly got to do_____ out best.__

We got-ta all___ pitch in, we got-ta do our thing,___ make a bet-ter world to live in, live___ in, live.___ Ev-'ry-bod-y let's___ sing, let's sing, let's___ sing. 'Bod-y let's

Ev - 'ry-bod-y let's a - sing, let free - dom ring, —

— let it ring, _____ let it _____ ring. _____

58

make a bet - ter world live in, live___ in.

PAPA WAS A RASCAL

By JAMES BOOKER

way with my pa - pa from old I - tal - ian Sal.

She stole a - way with my pa - pa a - way from old I - tal - ian Sal.

Yeah.

I was a young boy, a - bout the

age of nine. I found a sweet Rus - sian wo-man, you know I

made her mine. I found a sweet Rus - sian wo-man, you

know   that   I   made   her   mine.___

And then my

out for the C. I. A._____ Well, we

all got to watch out, watch out for the C. I. A._____ Yeah,_____

yeah,_____ yeah.

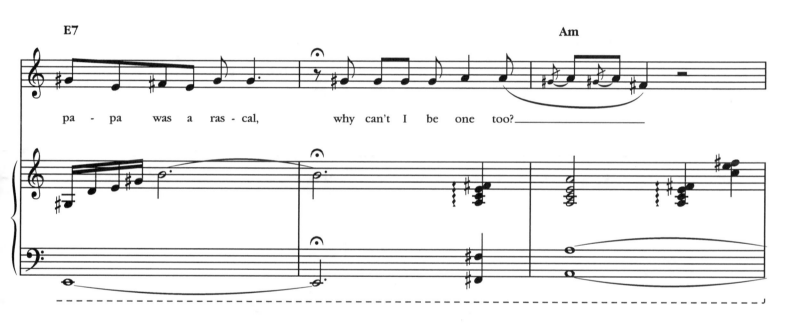

think I'm gon-na be____ one too.____

PIXIE

Words and Music by JAMES BOOKER

Ab7

Eb7

POP'S DILEMMA

By JAMES BOOKER

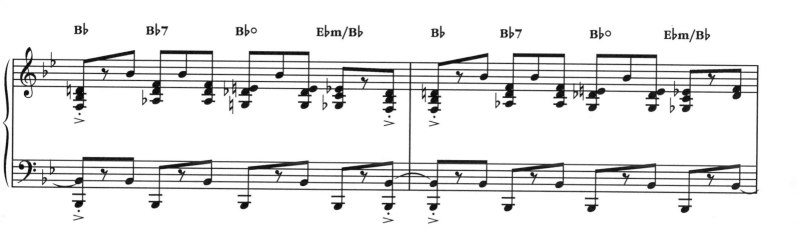

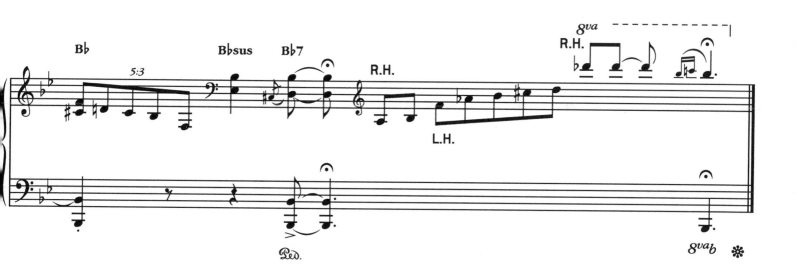

PUT OUT THE LIGHT

By JAMES BOOKER

TELL ME HOW DO YOU FEEL

Words and Music by PERCY MAYFIELD
and RAY CHARLES

Tell me how do you feel when your

ba - by's lov - in' your best friend?____ I wan-na know.____ Tell me how____

___ do you____ feel____ when your ba-by's lov - in' your best friend?____ I wan - na know.___

___ Do you feel like go - in' cra - zy, or do you feel you've al - ways been?__

well,   well a - well,   well a - well._____

124

MEDLEY
BLUES MINUET
IT WILL HAVE TO DO UNTIL THE REAL THING COMES ALONG
BABY, WON'T YOU PLEASE COME HOME

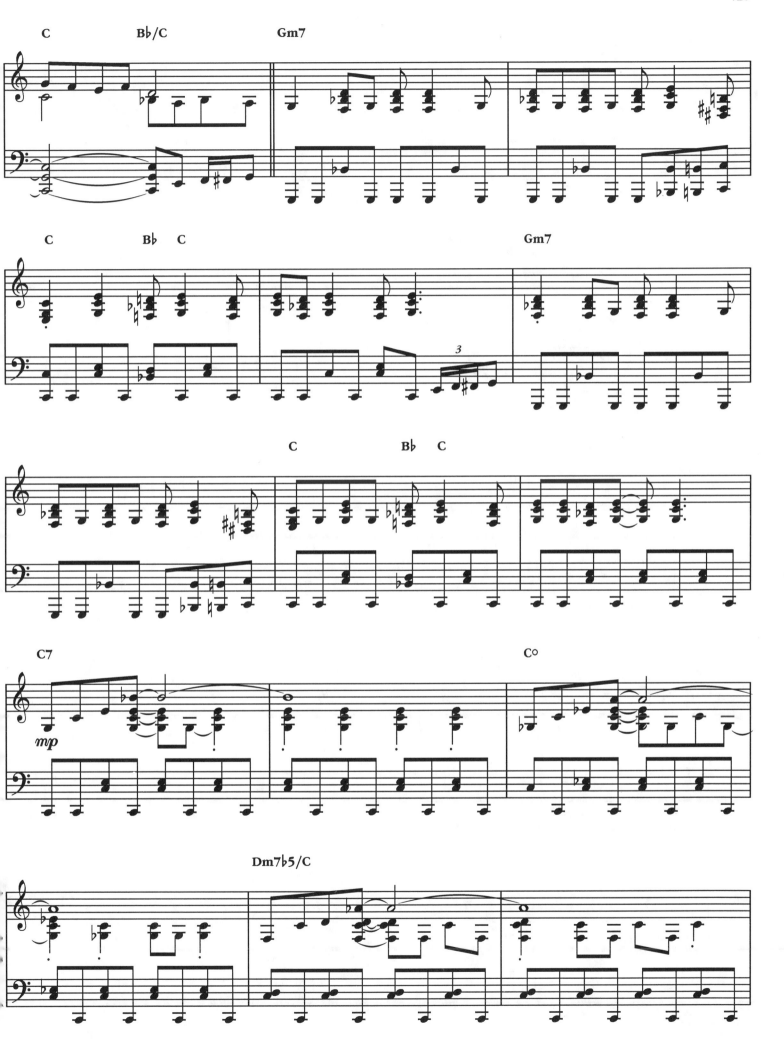

131

ba - by, won't you please come home?

Be-cause you dad - dy's all a-lone.

You know I've cried in vain,

nev-er more____ to

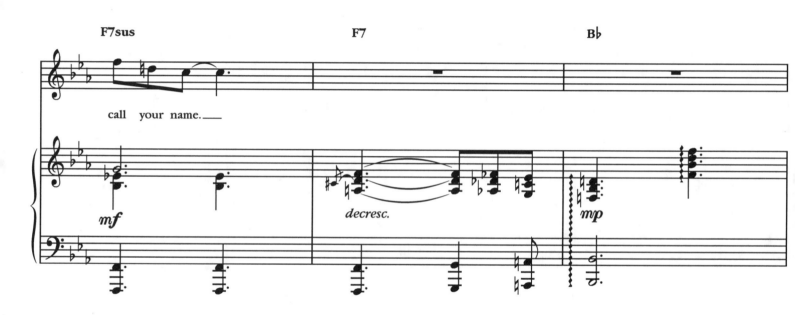

call your name.____

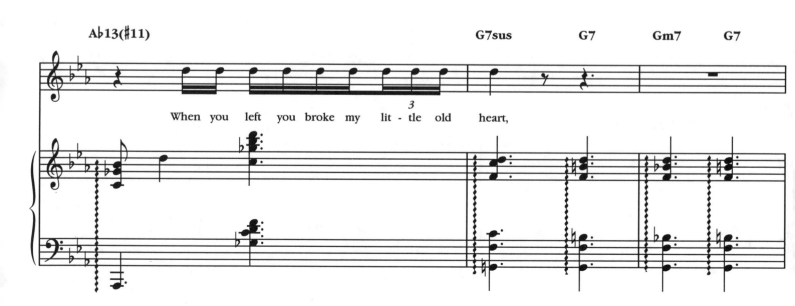

When you left you broke my lit-tle old heart,

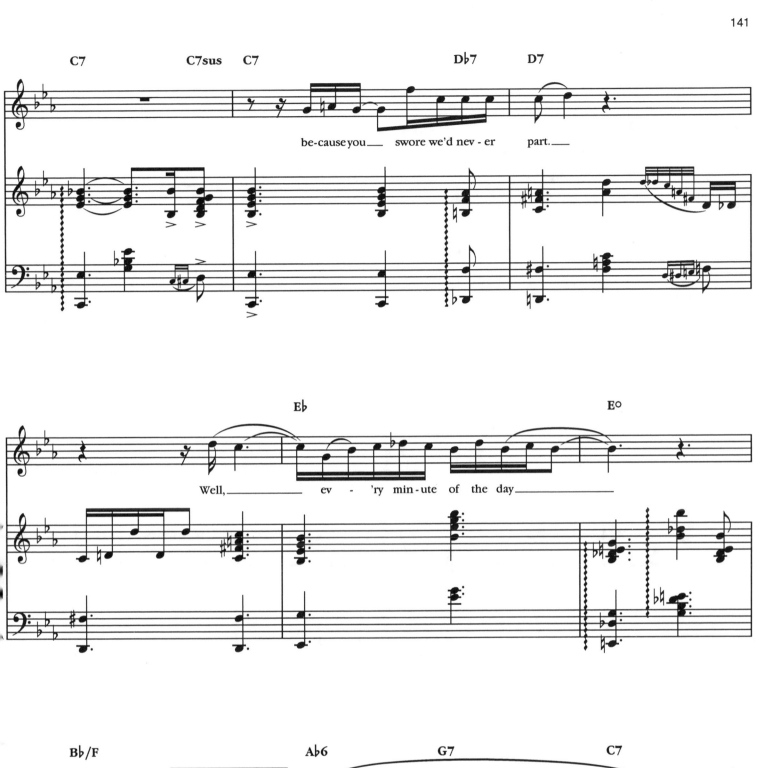

be-cause you____ swore we'd nev - er part.____

Well,_____ ev - 'ry min - ute of the day_____

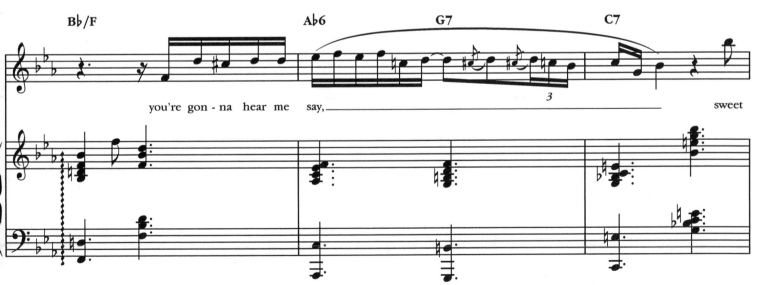

you're gon - na hear me say,_____ sweet

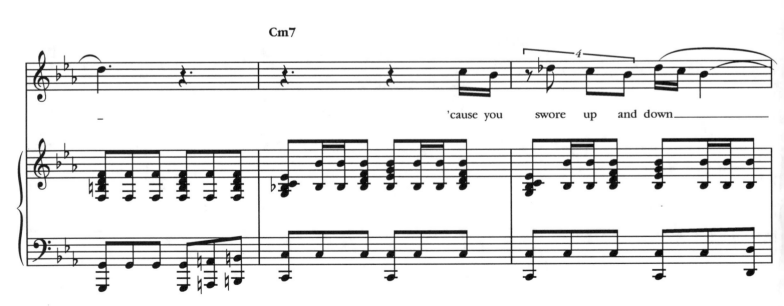